A LEADER'S STUDY GUIDE TO

The Gold Mine

The Gold Mine: a novel of lean turnaround, by Freddy and Michael Ballé, is an attempt to capture the human challenges facing leaders in a lean transformation. The company in this story is fortunate to work with a sensei. A true sensei (taken from the Japanese for teacher, or in this case master) does more than simply teach. He or she makes sure that lean leaders and team members stay on the straight and narrow path of lean outcomes, and avoid politics, rationalizations, or other human obstacles. Above all, a sensei helps generate the continuing lean discussion at the heart of continuous improvement. Indeed, this is why *The Gold Mine* was written as a novel: it highlights the nature of the human interaction beyond the cold dry facts of lean principles and tools. Learning lean has far more to do with emotion and behavior than simple cognition.

This study guide is designed to help lean practitioners who do not have access to a lean sensei. It seeks to generate collective reflection, or in lean terms, *hansei*. Author Jeffrey Liker says hansei "is not simply a philosophical belief system at Toyota, but a practical tool for improvement." The practice of hansei can help you confront your experiences with the stories told in the book so as to deepen your understanding. This process should help you to develop the critical insight to see a problem and then apply lean tools as a solution. As easy as this may sound, many people try to apply the tools without doing the upfront thinking first.

As you discuss the principles of lean that are uncovered in *The Gold Mine*, keep a few points in mind:

Lean is a system. Lean is far more than a toolbox of techniques. It's a system in which each tool is linked to all others according to fundamental principles. One of the key roles of a sensei is to make sure practitioners don't get so enamored with their favorite tool that they forget to keep their bearings on both the purpose of the tools (visualize problems and solve them), and the links with all the other tools (how often do you hear of successful tool changeover reduction without reduction of batch size?).

Lean is a practice, not just a philosophy. Learning only occurs by doing, and lean happens at the kaizen focal point, when something in the system is changed to reduce waste. The senseis constantly reinforce this practical blend: learn to see, take action, compare results, reflect, and take the next required steps. It is part of their job to be impatient with talk and concepts, with over-cautious plans, and to constantly remind practitioners of genchi genbutsu: go and see for yourself, and then, just do it. This aspect of the sensei's teaching is best conveyed by stories and vignettes in the lean tradition, which form the underlying basis for *The Gold Mine*. Every situation in the book is based on a sensei anecdote or story taken from the oral tradition of lean.

Lean is fundamentally about knowledge gained from rigorous problem-solving. Indeed, the sensei's role is to push the lean practitioner not to be satisfied with the first answer that comes to mind, but always to explore the question further, experiment, and ultimately learn, so as to continuously improve systems and operations.

So please put *The Gold Mine* to work. This study guide is designed to help working groups to explore and apply lean principles, regardless of where you may currently be on your own lean journey. This guide presents a summary and the key challenges in each of the book's chapters. The discussion points and resources that follow are selected to support further team discussion and learning. At the end of the guide you will find a lexicon of relevant lean terms. The Ballés recommend that you read one chapter a week, and meet to discuss its principles and to explore the key questions. Keep in mind that no one company will find an exact "fit" in terms of industry, or situation, or level of mastery: the point is to learn by reflecting on the experience shared in this story.

The Ballés' experience with numerous lean turnarounds (both sustained and failed) revealed to them that successful lean managers get obsessed with lean. They continually talk about lean, they explain everyday occurrences in terms of muda, flow, and takt; and they spend far more time on the shop floor driving lean than they do dealing with corporate politics. While this guide can never substitute for such gemba learning, it can help you take the next step forward on your path to perfection.

Chapter One

PROFIT IS KING, BUT CASH RULES

CHAPTER SUMMARY

Phil Jenkinson is a young entrepreneur with a struggling business. Despite healthy products, his company faces a serious cash crisis. And so he meets his sensei, Bob Woods. Bob is a retired automotive executive who has led many successfully automotive supplier turnarounds, yet has turned his back on industry to return to his first love of boats and sailing. Bob is brought back into the lean turnaround game by his son, Mike, who wants nothing to do with industry, but as Phil's best friend is convinced that his father's know-how and experience can help Phil save his company. Like many senseis, Bob initially rejects the notion that he should get involved. Eventually, however, he listens to Phil explain his problems, which show up as insufficient productivity and high inventory despite growing sales, all of which are now conspiring to create a cash crisis that is pushing the company to the brink of bankruptcy. Phil laments that his company is close to defaulting on its payments to suppliers, and can't pay back the high interest the banks are charging for the debts Phil and his partner guaranteed when they bought the ailing company.

The underlying challenge in this chapter is to understand the true nature of the crisis. In this case, it's neither a problem of sluggish sales, nor Phil's diagnosis of low profitability (although there is some of that). The primary culprit is poor cash flow due to low inventory turns and high cost of goods sold. The company has extremely poor output. If it could simply sell more products (and they do have a backlog of orders) without increasing overhead or labor cost, it could postpone the immediate risk of collapse and begin to turn around its prospects.

DISCUSSION POINTS

Before moving into the details of lean, it is important to have an overall grasp of the business challenge you're facing. Companies often treat a fleeting symptom, such as defects in one product or challenges training employees in a new policy, as the primary problem when in fact their core challenge lies deeper. So at the outset of any serious lean initiative, the participants must develop a shared understanding of the key challenge facing them. So ask yourself, as a fundamental beginning point for your lean journey:

What is your fundamental business challenge?

RESOURCE

Ohno, Taiichi. 1988. *The Toyota Production System: Beyond Large-Scale Production*. Portland, OR: Productivity Press.

After retiring from Toyota, lean pioneer Ohno wrote this appealing series of essays that give a high-level explication of Toyota's system. Don't expect a set of actions to put into practice on Monday morning from this book—yet Ohno provides fascinating insights into such topics as how Toyota developed the system in response to its post-World War II resources and abilities, and what it consciously adapted from Henry Ford. While many of the "Ohno stories" that Bob Woods tells may be apocryphal, they are often told and retold in the lean community for teaching purposes. This delightful book clarifies many core TPS concepts, and gives an insight into Ohno's character and outlook.

By providing a vivid history of TPS, Ohno explains the particular context in which it evolved, which is another way of explaining the specific problem the system was designed to address:

Needs and opportunities are always there. We just have to drive ourselves to find the practical ones. What are the essential needs of business under slow growth conditions? In other words, how can we drive productivity when the production quantity is not increasing?

Chapter Two

GOLD IN THE FLOW

CHAPTER SUMMARY

Phil and Mike drag a reluctant Bob to the factory, where he shows them how to quickly evaluate the efficiency of a factory by observing ongoing operations. Phil eventually convinces Mike's father to help out, on the condition that Bob won't have to deal with any politics. If people don't do as he says, Bob warns, he will take a walk. Phil eagerly accepts, and they return to the plant, where they are joined by Amy Cruz, the firm's HR manager. Bob teaches them to see what he calls the "gold in the flow," or the potential value lying dormant in the plant. By carefully tracking the flow of materials and work involved in making different products, they identify the various wastes in the process and see how this affects the performance of the plant. They then focus on a specific area and look at the key metrics of quality, productivity and inventory on that part of the process, and discuss the kind of targets for improvement on this line.

The challenge here is to visualize the entire flow of materials and information through the factory, and to realize that every product that gets held up because of waste reduces the contribution of all the fixed costs of the plant to profitability. Similarly, the company is penalized by every product not shipped to the customer, which counts as inventory that is being financed by the company (parts cost, labor content, holding and handling costs).

DISCUSSION POINTS

At this early stage, Bob is basically trying to open Phil's eyes, to see his shop floor as a flow of value that is broken by many obstacles that reduce productivity and erode cash flow. Seeing the shop floor in this manner is a key lean skill. Without it, you are prone to implement lean tools as isolated improvements instead of parts of an integrated system. In practice, of course, learning to see is challenging in one's own plant, where old habits, politics, and other human considerations often blind us to the real work. So ask yourself if you can "see" the process by which you create value for your customer.

Can you trace the value stream all the way from raw material through production and into the arms of the customer? And more importantly: what problems have been revealed as a result? What factors are causing value not to flow?

RESOURCE

Rother, Mike, and John Shook. 1998. *Learning to See: Value Stream Mapping to Add Value and Eliminate Muda*. Cambridge, MA: Lean Enterprise Institute, Inc.

This detailed workbook represents an excellent introduction to value-stream mapping. Rother and Shook share both the principles, and the practice, of diagramming every step involved in the material and information flows needed to bring a product from order to delivery. While Bob Woods introduces the notion of value-stream mapping only after he has determined that Phil and Amy have developed a gemba attitude later in the book, other lean senseis emphasize this way of thinking earlier in the teaching process. For readers looking to figure out where the gold is being held up in their processes, this workbook is the best place to start.

The authors make it clear that developing a mapping proficiency is as much about spotting waste as it is about tracking how well materials flow through the value stream.

Value-stream mapping is a pencil and paper tool that helps you to see and understand the flow of material and information as a product makes its way through the value stream. What we mean by value-stream mapping is simple: Follow a product's production path from customer to supplier, and carefully draw a visual representation of every process in the material and information flow. Then ask a set of key questions and draw a "future-state" map of how the value should flow.

Doing this over and over is the simplest way—and the best way we know—to teach yourself and your colleagues how to see value and, especially the sources of waste. Practice drawing value-stream maps and you will learn to see your shop floor in a way that supports lean manufacturing. Just remember that the point of getting lean is not "mapping," which is just a technique. What's important is implementing a value-adding flow. To create this flow you need a "vision" of the flow. Mapping helps you see and focus on flow with a vision of an ideal, or at least improved, state.

Chapter Three

TAKT TIME

CHAPTER SUMMARY

In order to ascertain a realistic target for headcount reduction on the mechanism line, Bob asks Phil to time the operators as they work. Yet the mere mention of stopwatches triggers angry resistance from Dave Koslowsky, the factory's production manager, which leads to Bob walking out, as promised. Amy charms Bob into accepting a compromise, in which he continues to talk to Phil and herself, on his turf, at the yacht club, and to give them homework from there. Bob then explains how building to customer demand, according to takt time, is the key to understanding the productivity problem. He teaches them how to ascertain the target number of operators that should be on the line. He also explains that the first step to lean improvement is basic process stability, and in the case of an assembly line, stopping defects in the process. He suggests a "red bin" system to isolate non-conformity at every workstation. He adds to this by discussing the impact of variation in the customer cycle on productivity, and advises them to start reducing the variation in the operators' cycle before tackling more detailed inefficiency.

The theme of this chapter is to understand the impact of one type of variation (quality) on process performance. There are two core points. The first is understanding takt time, which should be the North Star to regulate production processes, and is often misunderstood during lean implementations. The second is to use the process of calculating the target number of workers to train yourself to identify variation on the line. This will enable you to move on to analyzing your value-added work versus non-value added work. Keep in mind that to the worker, all activity is work, whether value added or not. Variation, however, caused either by man, machine, material, or method is a major problem regarding performance and must be dealt with.

DISCUSSION POINTS

While there are several key challenges posed in this chapter, start with this simple query:

Where—and how—are you producing waste?

Do you react immediately to correct the casue of this waste every single time we find an example? Remember, the point of this exercise is not simply to identify waste, but to train yourselves to eliminate it permanently.

As a starting point try the following exercise. With your team, develop a list of items that reveal waste. How can you tell, just by seeing and without asking any questions, how well the plant is operating? Then, pick a product and follow it through the plant or office, noting where inventory builds up, finished pieces sit unnecessarily, defects are built in, and so forth. Consider how often your work produces examples of the seven wastes:

1. overproduction of parts beyond customer demand
2. waiting of the operator
3. transport of parts or components
4. unnecessary processing
5. inventory of parts at the workstation
6. motion of the operator
7. non-conformities and rework

You can use your discoveries from this exercise as a starting point for kaizen work. Remember that you have *created* this waste through flawed process. Now that you have identified it, you can use the following methods to eliminate the systemic causes of muda.

Takt time, which figures prominently in the chapter under discussion, represents a key area to start: What is the takt time of the line or cell your team is focusing on? (This can be the same product family identified in the mapping exercise) Over how many weeks have you averaged the customer demand to calculate the takt time? How many shifts are you taking into account? What are the main sources of process instability on this cell or line?

In exploring these questions, you will gain a finer understanding of what is truly working, and what isn't, on the gemba. Operators should note unreliable equipment which has never been fixed by maintenance or engineering; spot non-conforming components which have to be reworked before they can be used; and identify material handling glitches which cause waiting, additional storage, and transport. In an office or other setting, this disciplined analysis will reveal examples of unnecessary work and rework, systemic failures to close loops, and overlapping and often varying forms and procedures.

RESOURCE

Rother, Mike, and Rick Harris. 2001. *Creating Continuous Flow: An Action Guide for Managers, Engineers, and Production Associates.* Cambridge, MA: Lean Enterprise Institute, Inc.

This workbook explains, in simple step-by-step terms, how to introduce and sustain lean flows in pacemaker cells and lines. A sequel to *Learning to See*, this workbook shows how to move from seeing how work and materials are organized to setting a production rhythm and applying the principles of continuous flow. This is an essential guide for the type of work that Amy and Phil tackle when redesigning the production cells and lines.

In particular, this guide explains why producing to takt time in a continuous flow is tied so strongly to identifying waste:

Lean manufacturing strives to achieve continuous flow in even greater measure, because it is the most efficient way of turning materials into products:

- *Minimum resources are used. The amount of people (direct and indirect), machines, materials, buildings, handling equipment, etc., required to make a product is kept to a minimum. This means higher productivity and lower costs.*

- *Shortened lead times, which permits quicker response to the customer and a shorter "money conversion cycle" (time between paying for raw material and getting paid for the products made out of those raw materials.)*

- *Problems such as defects can quickly become apparent instead of remaining hidden. Problems can be identified quickly and corrected before proceeding. It is easier to identify root causes of abnormalities when they are detected as they occur.*

- *Encourages communication between operations, which become linked in "customer-supplier" relationships.*

Any item produced before it is actually needed by the next processing step creates waste, such as extra handling, counting, storage and so on. When you see batching of even one extra piece, you should realize that you have used an operator's time to process and handle an item that was not needed. You could have used that person's time and skills to process something that was needed!

Chapter Four

STANDARDIZED WORK

CHAPTER SUMMARY

Phil, Amy and Mike meet up with Bob, who is busy clearing out the hold of his yacht to prepare for a new coat of paint. This leads to a discussion about standardized work, which is defined as always doing the same operations in the same order, and employing the Five S exercise. Phil and Amy are surprised to hear Bob's unusual take on Five S as the starting point of standardization and people involvement.

There's a key takeaway in this chapter: after takt time, standardized work is the second foundation of lean practice, one that is all too often obscured by the glamour of flow, kanban, and other exotic terms. Repeating the same operations in the same order absolutely needs to be understood by all in order to secure the lean gains beyond the initial kaizen workshops. Mastering Five S on the shop floor is a fundamental starting point of a process, which eventually leads to autonomous teams. It is not a mere "clean your room" tool, but rather, the core starting point to involve operators and generate suggestions. As such, Five S should never be underestimated.

DISCUSSION POINTS

Use a discussion—or better yet a practice—of the Five S exercise to assess standardization in your workplace. This understanding can be gleaned from the following question:

How well is the work defined, and how rigorously does the team focus on doing the same activities in the same sequence?

Discuss the impact of non-standardization on your every day factory and/or office environment and find the most glaring cases of waste. Remember that standardized work is dynamic because the standard is always being improved; it's creative, and not just following routine.

RESOURCE

Liker, Jeffrey, and Meier, David, 2006. *The Toyota Way Fieldbook: A Practical Guide for Implementing Toyota's 4Ps*. New York, NY: McGraw-Hill.

This comprehensive guide to implementing lean represents one of the most practical and wide-ranging resources for students. Far beyond any description of specific tools, this workbook strives to give a feel for what TPS is really about. Blending stories with charts, tips, and exercises, the fieldbook sheds light into many lesser-described aspects of TPS, such as the development of people through constant problem-solving. Phil and Amy could certainly benefit from such a discussion, particularly chapter six of this resource, "Establish Standardized Processes and Procedures."

This chapter explains why standardized work forms the basis for kaizen. In addition to providing strategies and tips for establishing standardized processes and procedures, the authors clarify why it matters:

The work of developing standards begins early in a lean implementation and is a common thread throughout the development of lean operations. The creation of standardized processes is based on defining, clarifying (making visual), and consistently utilizing the methods that will ensure the best possible results. As such, standardization is not applied as a stand-alone element at specific intervals. Rather, it is part of the ongoing activity of identifying problems, establishing effective methods, and defining the way those methods are to be performed. And it is driven by people, not done to people. People doing the work understand it in sufficient detail to make the biggest contributions to standardization.

Chapter Five

IT'S ALL ABOUT PEOPLE

CHAPTER SUMMARY

In this chapter, Phil and Amy find themselves both exhilarated and disturbed by what they've learned running workshops. They've discovered that, first, quick results are in fact easy to obtain by working with the operators. Second, they've found out that the operators have been complaining about causes of variation in their work for years, yet because management never paid attention, they have lowered their expectations of them. Phil and Amy want to build on the gains obtained from the workshops in day-to-day operations. Bob's third key concept of sustaining lean, after takt time and standardized work, is kaizen. To introduce it, Bob invites Phil, Amy and Mike to join him at the Yacht Club for the preparation of the first spring regatta. He shows them how the best skipper operates and details the key roles of supervisors and team leaders in sustaining lean. And he reveals the heart of the system: "it's all about people."

This chapter shows how the greatest challenges in lean truly involve people. Shifting supervisors from their traditional role of looking for missing parts and ad hoc rescheduling of people and production, to a mentoring job of developing work standards and training operators to work at the standard, is a fundamental lean leap. Indeed, one of the critical issues all lean companies face, Toyota included, is a constant dearth of good supervisors. Bob also defines the team leader role, which is an operator, not part of the hierarchy, for every team of five to seven operators, who makes sure hourly production targets are achieved by solving all the little mishaps which can happen in day-to-day operations and create variations in the work cycle. Overall, Bob's insight in lean management is that you have to "produce people before producing parts."

17

DISCUSSION POINTS

Use the themes of this chapter to explore the role and actions of supervisors and line workers. One of the secrets of sustaining lean improvement is investing in enough management and technicians to resolve problems as they appear on the gemba, rather than simply listing them as priorities set by management in their offices. This investment in shop-floor leadership pays for itself in spectacular productivity gains. The primary question raised is:

Are supervisors truly involved with work standards and daily shop-floor improvement?

Examine this topic through questions such as: How much support do our front-line people really get? When a machine is stopped, or a defect appears, or a problem arises with a customer being served, do we see shop-floor management and/or technicians come running? Are operators ever left to fend for themselves with technical problems? Are supervisors focused on solving operators' problems rather than ordering them about? An interesting shop floor exercise for your supervisors is to ask them daily: "What have you done to help operators reach their targets today?"

Above all, simply having this discussion should raise and explore some fundamental questions about how well the team leaders are supporting the workers. The way in which individuals grapple with the questions should shed light into how well they are being empowered to be problem solvers, and how well management works with the workers to identify and solve problems.

RESOURCE

Liker, Jeffrey. 2004. *The Toyota Way: 14 Management Principles from the World's Greatest Manufacturer.* New York, NY: McGraw-Hill. An excellent, detailed book that combines a thorough reporting of Toyota's practices with an insightful codification of the company's practices. Liker's deep knowledge of Toyota's practice over the past 20 years brings extra rigor to his explanation of the principles, and reveals the essence of its managerial system better than any other text to date. This book answers Phil's questions about the core principles of TPS, providing a different focus than that of Bob Woods. This resource will help keep you focused on the right managerial practices by making the underlying principles explicit.

Here's how Liker limns the basis, for example, of deeply observing and then solving problems at the source:

The practice of genchi genbutsu is easy to adopt as a corporate policy and new hires can be sent out to the shop floor to "go and see" and then report back on what they see. But at Toyota, this is not simply a lesson for the neophyte to learn. The executive or manager must go, see, and really understand the actual situation at the working level. Managers are not just managing technology or tasks; they are promoting the culture. The absolute core of the Toyota philosophy is that the culture must support the people doing the work. Management must demonstrate a commitment to quality every day, but ultimately quality comes from the workers.

Chapter Six

LEVEL TO PULL

CHAPTER SUMMARY

Now that Mike, Phil, and Amy have enjoyed significant results on the mechanisms sub-assembly lines in terms of increasing daily production with the same resources, while consistently hitting the new production targets, Bob drags them to the local supermarket to see how pull works on an entire flow. The first important pull concept is the "shop stock," or supermarket. Work-in-process, or WIP, should be held at the cell as output from the process as opposed to being held as material and components waiting to be transformed, since lean processes always stress flow over storing excess material.

This leads Amy to draw a parallel from her experience working in a fast food restaurant, most of which have a shop stock behind the counter. This inventory contains several rows of standard burgers for the "runners," models most people are likely to purchase because they are basic standards. When one of these burgers is sold at the counter, the salesperson tells the production staff to make another; or in other words, the counter pulls stock replenishment in the burgers' shop stock. The advantage of this system is that customers ordering standards can be served in a few seconds by helping them from the stock; and that if several customers want the same type of burger at the same time, they are all held in the buffer. Also, the rotation prevents burgers from going stale. At low traffic periods, the shop stock is often kept empty.

The system is lean because it pulls on a controlled stock and delivers goods to customers just-in-time, while the staff resources in the kitchen vary according to the demand at various hours of the day. In industry, flow can be complicated by the fact that changeovers are hardly ever instantaneous, so batching might be a necessary evil. And so Bob explains how to use takt time to build a leveled production program, which pulls continuously on the production cell as with the burger stand. Later, at a dinner party with a lean academic specialist, he details to Phil the link between pull, leveling and tool changeover.

The key challenge in this chapter is getting a feel for pull production as opposed to push production. It is important to realize that for a just-in-time system to deliver lean results in terms of labor cost and capital utilization, the pull signal must be "leveled" as much as can be, both in mix and volume. This is a critical lean insight to gain, because without it your team will never be able to reap the cash, labor and capital benefits from just-in-time techniques such as kanban.

DISCUSSION POINTS

As you explore the details of push and pull production, or even the finer nuances of Steve McAllister's "square, circles, and triangles" demonstration as a way of understanding the dual implications of reducing batch size and increasing internal delivery in order to reduce WIP, focus on the idea of creating level pull. Have all your discussions to date given you the ability to track products along the value stream, identifying waste and standardizing operations, so that you can now pace the production and ensure "pull"?

Does the work flow, and is it regulated by the pace of customer demand?

RESOURCE

Smalley, Art 2004. *Creating Level Pull: A Lean Production System Improvement Guide for Production Control, Operations, and Engineering Professionals.* Cambridge, MA: Lean Enterprise Institute

This excellent workbook shows how to continue the lean transformation from a handful of isolated improvements to an entire level, pull-based system. As Amy and Phil are learning, implementing lean ideas beyond point optimization and flow in just one value stream requires conducting system kaizen to create a lean production system that ties together the flow of information and materials supporting every product family in a facility. Even Bob Woods tends to focus only on one of Phil's products when explaining pull, although he mentions other elements of the system. This guide works through the details of facility-wide pull systems in an instructive manner and clearly addresses the thorny issues of leveling in mix and volume.

Achieving this state is no easy task, as Smalley points out:

Continuous flow of materials and products in any production is a wonderful thing, and lean thinkers strive to create this condition wherever possible. The reality of manufacturing today and for many years to come, however, is that disconnected processes upstream will feed activities downstream. Additionally, many internal processes are currently batch-oriented and function as shared resources. The major challenge in this situation is for downstream processes to obtain precisely what they need when they need it, while making upstream activities as efficient as possible. This is where leveled demand and pull production are critical.

Chapter Seven

KANBAN RULES

CHAPTER SUMMARY

Phil and Amy badger Bob into returning to the factory, where he compliments them briefly about their progress before pointing out all they've done wrong. This starts a new round of discussion about how to establish a kanban, as well as a discussion of basic kanban rules, and more importantly, an inquiry into a kanban's true purpose. Bob tries to clarify by asking them to visualize the entire flow in the plant, from the truck preparation area in dispatch, to the shop stock at the conveyor and at the mechanism lines. He also introduces the heijunka board, which tells the material handler how to do the picking from the conveyor's shop stock into the truck preparation area. Amy and Phil complain about the difficulties they are experiencing with Kevin Lorenz, the plant's logistics manager.

A couple of weeks later, Bob accepts an invitation to return to the factory once more when Phil and Amy hit a wall. This visit leads to a loud argument with Lorenz, who ends up being publicly humiliated by Bob's friend Harry, who suggests to Phil that he should fire Lorenz right then and there. After everyone calms down, Bob admits that the plant is not progressing as fast as it should, particularly on the inventory front, and takes the blame for not being more involved. He has tried to advise at arms length, which can't work with lean transformation. In the end, Bob will have to return more often to the shop floor to help Phil and Amy with their lean implementation.

The key challenge in this chapter is to see lean flow as a logistics issue as well as a production one. Production needs to be stabilized, which will only happen if logistics maintains a steady pull on the production cells and regularly supplies the cells with the needed components and materials. On the shop floor, leveled pull is realized by the heijunka board, or leveling board, which simulates the customer's use of the product in its own production line. Bob teaches them that kanban is a kaizen tool, not the other way round. That kanban was not invented to relieve production from worrying about logistics. On the contrary, kanban's purpose is to fail every time the flow gets out of standard conditions. Because no one wants the kanban to fail (which can stop the entire plant), shop-floor management must constantly make sure that production and logistics glitches are solved in real-time. Kanban is in fact a tool to schedule production in a way that problems will appear visually immediately, at the point of the problem, so that they can be resolved right away.

DISCUSSION POINTS

Is your team familiar with all the basics rules of kanban?

- The following process comes to withdraw from the preceding process.
- The preceding process only produces what has been withdrawn.
- Production or withdrawal only happens with corresponding kanban cards.
- No parts are allowed on the shop floor without a kanban attached to them.
- Zero defects in the parts delivered by the upstream process.
- Reduce the number of kanban over time.

Regardless of whether you work in an office or factory, the principles of kanban apply. Discuss each kanban rule with your team, and clarify its purpose. Talk about the broader purpose of kanban as an indicator of where the process is broken or suboptimal.

Can you draw out on paper a complete kanban loop with:

• Heijunka board
• Kanban posts
• Kanban waiting file

Are all members of your team clear on the difference between a production instruction kanban, and a withdrawal kanban? Can your kanban help standardize the flow of material and information throughout the plant or office?

Does your kanban reveal the sources of waste and the health of your processes? And how are you addressing the problems in topics such as delivery and flexibility?

RESOURCE

Harris, Rick, Chris Harris, and Earl Wilson. 2003. *Making Materials Flow: A Lean Material Handling Guide for Operations, Production Control, and Engineering Professionals.* Cambridge, MA: Lean Enterprise Institute, Inc.

This hands-on workbook teaches how to create continuous flow by supplying purchased parts to the value stream in an optimal manner. It builds on the lessons of *Creating Continuous Flow*, showing how, to quote from its foreword, "to create a circulatory system that takes full advantage of your carefully created areas of continuous flow while also meeting the needs of other production areas still in batch mode." This guide would come in handy to Phil and Amy as they try to sort out logistics toward the end of this story and address the new challenges exposed by the successes the company has created.

The authors spell out how this workbook helps lean practitioners build on their past successes:

Many facilities that are lean in terms of operating their individual processes are still mass producers in supplying these processes. They lack a Plan for Every Part (PFEP). (Indeed, some facilities seem to lack a plan for any part!) They lack a properly located and managed purchased-parts market. They lack a rigorous material delivery route using standard work. And they lack pull signals to tightly link their areas of continuous flow to the supply of materials. The consequence is starvation of processes, loss of flow, and a major waste of effort and money in keeping too much inventory and spending too much time hunting for missing items.

Chapter Eight

GEMBA ATTITUDE

CHAPTER SUMMARY

In this chapter, Bob shifts Phil and Amy's focus from the mechanics of flow and kanban back to the core of lean, which is attitude. He takes them back to the shop floor, pushing them to learn to see by looking intently at the equipment, and of course, at the operating conditions, which people create. Bob points out that beyond the usual tools, such as SMED and TPM, the heart of lean is rigorous problem-solving. Indeed, to obtain results after the initial quick wins from these tools, one must follow the five why exercise rigorously, so as to always resolve the fundamental cause of any problem. Secondly, Bob demonstrates the "just-do-it" element of the lean attitude in organizing an impromptu build of the cabinet assembly cell, working with the operators and shop-floor technicians. These shop-floor actions lead to another run-in with the plant's management structure and force Phil and Matt, his partner, to finally make a stand for or against total lean implementation.

The key point of this chapter is that while many try to lean their operations, few succeed. The authors believe that although people get mesmerized by the technicalities of lean tools such as kanban and leveling, they often completely miss several core principles of lean: never by-pass a problem and work with the operators to continuously improve operations. In that respect, this is probably the most important chapter of the book, and raises a fundamental issue for you to ponder: are you really walking the walk, or are you just talking the talk!

DISCUSSION POINTS

This chapter addresses the practical details of your lean implementation effort, and should prod you to examine the reality of your initiative. Remember, the "just-do-it" nature of lean means you should be doing lean rather than simply discussing it. And as this chapter reveals, tackling and even resolving difficult challenges only exposes new ones. And so you must set aside time to continually examine the quality of its efforts. Ask yourself: are our lean improvement initiatives as robust as the processes we are improving? How much time do we really spend simply looking at operations? Do we walk the gemba at the very least once a day to look at production boards and check the response time from technicians to operator problems? Do we hold all meetings at the gemba, with the real people in front of the real parts?

Finally, how committed are we to these efforts? Once we've achieved progress, is everyone willing to press forward? At this point, the question for your group is more of a challenge:

What was the last lean experiment we ran on our gemba and what did we learn from it?

RESOURCE

Ohno, Taiichi. 1988. *Workplace Management*. Portland, OR: Productivity Press.

In this modest and accessible series of short pieces, Ohno shares the most personal perspective of Toyota management. His essays range from historical pieces on Toyota's history as a weaving company to the application of TPS to white collar work, and all are based on his extensive experience and unshakeable belief that learning must be derived from direct observation.

This perspective certainly guides his teachings on the way that workplace supervisors must, for example, be seen doing very specific things as opposed to merely having a physical presence:

What you have to do is go into the plant and walk along at a rate of several hours per 100 meters. No one is going to rely on you as long as you cover those 100 meters rapidly.

"Why work standing up," you might ask a worker. "Nobody's going to complain if you're sitting down." If you have the worker use a certain tool sitting down because it is more comfortable that way, word will get around fast. People will talk about the supervisor who came along and showed them how to make their jobs easier. Then others will ask you to come take a look at their work stations. Pretty soon, you will have a hard time covering those 100 meters in the workplace.

Chapter Nine

THE HEIJUNKA WAY

CHAPTER SUMMARY

Phil faces a new unexpected problem as Bob informs him that his work is done. Now Phil must step up and manage the transformation. It's Phil's plant, and he should lead, or let it go. Phil reluctantly chooses to stay and lead the continued lean effort. Yet he also persuades Bob to continue to advise him, and asks Bob to state his vision of lean principles. Bob then explains the use of value stream mapping, or MIFA (Material and Information Flow Analysis.) Phil and Bob also discuss the tricky issues of leveling in volume as well as in mix, and understanding the relationship between JIT shop floor techniques and the MRP. They explore how to protect the production process from volume variations in customers' orders, and how to avoid passing on these variations to their suppliers, which would increase the likelihood of missing parts, and hence return variation in the production process.

The focus on this chapter is on management, and the need to maintain both a big picture outlook and a detailed vision of the plant at the same time. Bob helps Phil to visualize the plant's processes as a continuous flow, and enlarges the vision to include customer and supplier effects on the total supply chain.

DISCUSSION POINTS

In recent years, much has been made of value-stream mapping as a first step to lean transformation. Oddly enough, this is a well-known Toyota tool which the senseis often introduce late in their supplier plants they help, fearing the tool could become a distraction from genchi gembutsu: go and see. So be sure that your maps are serving the right purpose of focusing your attention on the work itself. And at this point, it's important to see the whole of the work, to see how the elements of the system relate and support one another, and to see the extended value streams in the workplace.

The key question here addresses the systematic impact of your lean efforts. Armed with the tools and principles discussed to date, take a step back and assess how well the system works as a whole. Ask yourself:

How are the different elements of our lean system supporting or hindering each other? And how is this overall system helping us to improve customer satisfaction?

RESOURCE

Womack, James, and Daniel Jones. 2002. *Seeing the Whole: Mapping the Extended Value Stream.* Cambridge, MA: Lean Enterprise Institute, Inc.

Learning to see, and to map, value streams, represents a powerful step in identifying and removing waste. But there's always room for improvement. This comprehensive guide teaches users of value-stream mapping how to extend this field of view beyond the facility level to see all the steps and time needed to bring a typical product from raw materials to finished goods. Now that Phil has begun to see the flow of value, this workbook would prove particularly handy as he continues to pursue lean with customers and suppliers.

As the authors point out:

Looking at the whole has always seemed natural to us and doing so will always suggest ways to slash costs while dramatically improving responsiveness and quality. Yet most managers we have encountered on our value stream walks want to stand in one place and look only at one point—their machine, their department, their plant, their firm. Often, the machine, the department, the plant, and the firm are performing well on traditional measures—high labor and machine utilization, low defects, on-time shipments—and the managers are pleased with their achievements.

However, when we get managers to change their focal plane from their assets and their organization to look at the product itself and what is actually happening on its long journey, they immediately realize that the performance of the entire value stream is abysmally suboptimal. Indeed, most wonder how they have worked for years in traditionally compartmentalized operations and somehow failed to notice the waste everywhere.

Chapter Ten

KAIZEN FOREVER

CHAPTER SUMMARY

Working life being what it is, Phil encounters a new round of challenges. Although he has had spectacular results in the lean turnaround of his plant, his managerial problems are mounting. Moving from lean production to creating a truly lean enterprise that can sustain shop-floor successes is no small task. Bob organizes a plant tour by his own sensei, visiting from Japan. The sensei seems to scarcely notice Phil's achievements, choosing instead to chastise him for ignoring quality concerns. This leads to a discussion about jidoka, the lesser known pillar of the Toyota Production System, and the various techniques associated with building quality into the products: andon, autonomation, poka-yoke, etc.

The overall message of this chapter is that the race to lean is unending. While Phil has reached a new level of performance, he now faces a new order of problems, which have been uncovered precisely by having sorted out the most obvious issues. In terms of lean maturity, this represents a coming of age for Phil. He realizes that the true secret of lean success is that, regardless of how expert one gets, every individual remains a student who must be open and devoted to continuing their lean voyage of discovery.

DISCUSSION POINTS

After reading *The Gold Mine*, and discussing it with your team, ask if you are truly ready to seek out a sensei to help you in your transformation. Seeking a sensei is not an admission of defeat. On the contrary, as this appears in every serious lean conversion, it is the first sign of real commitment. Seeking a sensei helps you sort out true lean wisdom from mere drivel. And the process will naturally bring your team in contact with the lean community at large, which will have increasing returns as true Lean Thinkers are always eager to share their successes and pass on free advice. So ask: who's your sensei? And more important, once you've established this, ask the most important question of all:

What's next?

RESOURCE

Womack, James, and Daniel Jones. 1996. *Lean Thinking: Banish Waste and Create Wealth in Your Organization*. New York: Simon & Schuster.

This fundamental resource, which popularized the principles of lean production to a broad audience, could just as easily serve as the first resource to consult for further learning. Yet the nature of lean's unending continuous improvement qualifies this book as an important ally at any point in a lean lesson. Spanning companies in different industries and countries, the authors draw from elaborate research to extract a handful of powerful principles that define lean practice. Extremely useful, especially to hold up against the definition of lean as proposed by Woods senior.

Here's how they explain the never-ending challenge that rewards even the most accomplished lean leaders:

Just as the introduction of lean thinking forces problems and waste to the surface in all operational areas, new organizational problems will inevitably arise as you apply these ideas. As you shrink your traditional functions, which were formerly the key to career paths in your organization, many employees will start to express anxieties about where they are going and whether they will have a 'home.' And as you place more employees in development and production activities relentlessly focused on the here-and-now, you may begin to wonder about their hard technical skills. Are your engineers retaining leading-edge capabilities or are they simply applying over and over what they already know?

Perhaps most striking, as you take all of the excess inventories and waste out of your internal value streams, you will become much more aware of the costs and performance problems of firms above and below you along the stream, including your suppliers' suppliers and your distributors' retailers. Offering them technical assistance will be necessary, but it won't be sufficient. To move farther down the path to leanness, it will soon be apparent that you will need to work with all the participants in a value stream in a new way.

LEAN IS A PRACTICE, NOT A THEORY

An interview by Tom Ehrenfeld with
Freddy and Michael Ballé, authors of *The Gold Mine*

Q. How does *The Gold Mine* fit in with existing literature that teaches lean thinking or change management?

A. The truth is that part of what makes lean difficult is the linkage between change management and the lean tools. Most books that tackle both lean thinking and change management tend to approach these subjects separately. First they'll describe the lean tools, and then they'll go into change management theory. With *The Gold Mine*, we've tried to deal with these two themes concurrently, progressing on both fronts at the same time.

This approach also addresses one of the reasons that it's so hard to find any workable lean "recipe," which is that the tools, or at least their level of implementation, must be linked to the management's lean maturity. For instance, we would argue that lean is fundamentally about rigorous problem solving and involving operators in kaizen. Fine. But in most working environments, if you start there, as most TQM or six sigma programs do, you will end up with disappointing results. People will get confused about which problems to solve, how to go about change, and what kind of attitude to adopt when dealing with resistance or recurring problems. In a factory it's usually easier to start a lean program with the basics, such as seven wastes, 5S, red bins for quality, reducing batch sizes by increasing tool changeovers, and moving progressively to eliminating variation in the operators' work cycle.

This is why senseis have a hard time giving the whole story upfront. They need to enable people to realize small and tangible results, which they can then build on. This is the only meaningful way to move forward. We've tried to capture this way of learning in *The Gold Mine*. It's a very different-and effective-approach to change management.

In fact, we had originally planned to write a book about lean and change management, but soon realized that precisely because it does not fit with the accepted theories of change management, we would end up with a heavily theoretical book trying to explain just what the senseis actually do, from a management practice point of view. In the end, we decided the tools and principles would be more accessible if we just tried to describe them in action.

Q. Are you saying that the experience of companies that embark on the path to lean differs from the models set out in the leading literature?

A. Not exactly. In fact, the model of value, flow, pull, perfection, and progression, articulated by Jim Womack and Dan Jones, certainly describes the way that most turnarounds that we've observed unfold. But very few of them start with a shared understanding among the workers of where they will eventually end up. The turnaround starts by increasing the tension in the system, and then resolving problems as they arise. This process will make the players start by defining value, and then solve the flow problems, move to pull and finally endlessly kaizen the process to perfection. So they do end up following this path. But it's virtually impossible for the change leaders to plan it as such, because you need to move from one practical implementation to another.

In fact, this marks another way that *The Gold Mine* differs from most change management literature. The story format treats both change and lean techniques concurrently. And the underlying change model, while characteristic of lean, challenges mainstream change management approaches in its dependence on the role of the sensei, who acknowledges progress, certainly, but also provides endless constructive criticism and challenge so that no one stops at the first results, but continues to improve endlessly.

In terms of lean thinking, we don't claim to add much to existing literature of lean tools. We have tried to present the techniques in a slightly different way, however, thereby helping readers see how the tools and principles are tied to one another. Firstly, we do try to point out that just-in-time and the flow techniques such as kanban, heijunka and pull, are only one pillar of the Toyota Production System (TPS), and we re-emphasize the lesser known jidoka pillar, which is equally important. Secondly, we strive to establish the links between the different elements of the system, such as kanban and jidoka. Kanban can't be successful if quality is not already under control, for example, or if employees aren't responsive to problems on the shop floor. A systematic study of the links felt like a daunting task, so we've used dialogue to point out the most obvious links to keep in mind when implementing the tools.

Finally, now that most of the tools are known and published, we've placed less emphasis on the tools per se, and more on their purpose within the lean system. Five S, for example, is not a "clean your room" technique, but a fundamental tool to work on standardization and employee involvement. In this respect, we believe we've occasionally highlighted different aspects of tools that have been already much discussed, and we believe that even the veteran lean practitioner can find food for thought in some of these discussions.

Q. Bob Woods, the gruff lean sensei of this book, stresses that the real challenge "is all about people." Can you explain? Are people issues more difficult to resolve than technical ones?

A. We find it hard to distinguish "technical" issues from "people" issues. Indeed, the two cannot be separated. And so the real question that matters is this: what does it take for lean to become part of the company's culture? The answer is: a critical mass of people who both think lean and act lean.

Regardless of how much has been published about the topic, thinking lean is not that obvious. Most people who observe their operations conclude that while they might understand this lean concept very well, it just doesn't apply to their particular circumstance. They need help in seeing the connection.

One of the most powerful insights from Womack and Jones is that lean is not simply a toolbox, but a total perspective. In other words, you must trust people to solve their problems, regardless of the way the problem has been defined. A plant manager, for example, typically defines a problem as: Hit your numbers, keep the factory loaded, and avoid too much union or vendor problems. This effectively forces him to stay in his office, manage by the numbers, run large batches and so on. A lean approach redefines the problem completely. His new goals would be: produce only what has been consumed (or ordered), never by-pass a problem or let an operator face a problem alone and continuously improve all processes. This has dramatic implications for the work of the same plant manager. The only way to solve problems in this lean perspective is to spend most of his or her time on the shop floor trying to understand what goes on, and challenging teams to be more precise and to improve their operations.

So the first real difficulty with lean deals with both technical and people challenges. The change begins by framing the problem, which one recognizes in the factory from a lean perspective.

Q. So how, then, do people actually get started on this approach?

A. They need to, in essence, develop a lean eye. John Shook and Mike Rother's book, Learning to See, refers to the genchi gembutsu, which is translated as "go see for yourself." *The Gold Mine* starts from this perspective. Before being exposed to lean ideas, Phil Jenkinson (a co-founder of the example company) has to learn to see his factory in much greater detail and understand how the different elements affect each other.

Developing this discipline remains an extraordinary challenge for all individuals, regardless of their background or the lean level of the plant. This is what folks call a moving target. Consider a plant that has managed to achieve pull, flow, with a supermarket after the cell, a truck preparation area, kanban, and so on. All's well. Right? Now, imagine that the material handler comes to pick up a container from the supermarket with a kanban card, but the box isn't there. The truck still needs to be prepared, so the system now tells her to get the container from the safety stock. This choice, however, would not be using the principle of pull correctly. The properly operating pull system would in fact create the right tension that forces the individual to solve the root cause-in this case, to determine what caused the container not to be there in the first place.

However, it takes a sensei level of lean observation to see beyond what appears to be happening in the flow. Most of us would be impressed by the technique of lean, the kanban, the supermarket, the truck preparation, and not see that all of this is failing to do what it's supposed to, which is solve the problems. So learning to see is a pretty big challenge, both on the technical and people front, at whatever lean level you are.

Q. What else is necessary to produce true change?

A. Realizing that "lean behavior" is a matter of doing as much as understanding. Most people need to understand an idea before they actually act upon it. Indeed, who can blame them? If someone starts with the assumption that they understand the concepts but don't believe they apply, they will never make any progress. This is tricky. In many cases, it's hard to see how the lean concepts presented in the literature apply to each industrial situation. Consider, for example, the whole issue of takt time and standardized work as raised in *The Gold Mine*. Standardized operator movements come pretty naturally at takt times around one to five minutes. Below that, it's too short, and over five, the cycles start getting long. The characters at IEV (Phil's company) have a ten minute takt time. In some industries, we could be in a two-hour takt time! So does that mean that standardized work does not work? Of course not. Rather, it means that the application of standardized work is not always so obvious. And each person must develop his or her own understanding of how to make the concept actually pay off. And the only way to gain this insight is to try it and see where you arrive.

A fundamental point about lean implementation is that "all things are never equal" in a factory. If you change one element of the system, chances are that you've changed how every other problem appears. We've tried to demonstrate this in *The Gold Mine*. Lean learning relies very strongly on the well-known body of knowledge known as "just do it." Beyond the basics on lean technique, the only way to learn is to try it out and see what happens. Practice, one hopes, makes perfect. But to do so, you must be in a controlled environment that enables you to see what is actually happening. Basic tools such as production analysis boards, red bins and 5S must be firmly in place.

Q. Phil Jenkinson, the company co-founder, seems constantly surprised and frustrated by the resistance he encounters to the turnaround. How realistic is his experience, and what should readers, managers, and leaders learn from this?

A. Our rule of thumb when writing the Phil character was that every plant manager who has tried lean transformation would think: Yep, I've been there. So, yes, we believe that Phil's experience is pretty realistic, although, of course, real-life plant managers will react very differently according to their own personality. Phil's greatest revelation might be that lean implementation ultimately requires a lean attitude. This speaks to the issue of resistance. One of the first things a lean sensei told us was that the greatest weakness of lean was exclusive reliance on the plant managers. True-but, interestingly, we've also come to believe that this very trait is one of the keys of the effectiveness of lean. You can transform your company culture to benefit from lean by creating a critical mass of the right people.

So the key issue is: what proportion of your employees, from top management to operators are lean converts? Pragmatically, there are only two ways of changing this proportion: either you convince people or you replace them, which is exactly the problem Phil is facing in *The Gold Mine*. As we've tried to show in the novel, it's not an easy issue and should not be dealt with by knee-jerk reactions. In the book, the resistant production manager later becomes a key asset, and so on, but, fundamentally to us the core lean implementation issue is: how do you maintain a high proportion of lean converts in your teams, and how do you continuously challenge them to go further in lean, and not rest at their current level of achievement?

There's another intriguing element to the way in which lean change occurs over time. In hindsight, many participants are surprised to realize that just about every lean concept or practice strikes them as "common sense." When people experience the moment at which they suddenly "get it," they will just about slap their forehead and say, "of course" as they then see the implications. A plant manager with the epiphany realizes that stocks are better held after the process in a supermarket (as in pull), rather than before the process in the form of components or material (as in push). A maintenance manager who "gets it" suddenly realizes that, yes, the only sure way of knowing why a machine is down half the time, or produces bad parts, is to stand in front of it watching it cycle until understanding what makes it break down or produce scrap. These are very emotional moments, and we've witnessed many.

These "a-ha" moments are the key to people expanding their understanding of lean. Phil experiences several epiphanies in the book (in his case, they mostly deal with standardization). People who experience one of these "turn-on-the-light-bulb" moments almost always assume that everyone around them also sees this astounding common sense. And so they end up being taken aback by the resistance. The problem is that you can't manufacture a-ha's with the same precision and predictability as you do parts. Each individual has a different point-of-view and history, and generating these insights are an outcome of larger realignments in perspective. They tend to happen one person at a time, one idea at a time. And sometimes only after years of explanations of the same simple idea over and over, such as the formula that margin = price - cost as opposed to price = cost + margin.

Q. If lean is all about seeking perfection, why don't the characters appear to be more happy as they travel the path?

A. Frustration is a common feeling for plant managers engaged in a lean transformation. There are many practical reasons. First, lean results seldom happen in isolation. In order to have a workable kanban system, for example, you must have already achieved some traction in production, logistics, and quality. Every single little action takes a whole lot of convincing, which can be very frustrating. Managers often feel that they spend far more time explaining or twisting arms than actually doing lean. Of course, that's just part and parcel of the process.

Secondly, even when people are engaged and on board, transformation feels like an agonizingly slow process simply because it's such hard work! Reducing tool change, for example, is easy during a single minute exchange of die (SMED) workshop where you often get 40% to 50% reduction with no sweat. But it's a lot harder to obtain shorter tool changes systematically at every change. And then to conduct tool change from last good part to first good part. Taking on comprehensive tasks such as reducing bad start-up parts can be a real headache. It takes a lot of hard work in some cases, to find the pixies in the system, and actually solve problems.

This frustration can be all the stronger when a company has committed resources to lean transformation. In the early phases, when the leaders are getting the basics in place, any pressure for immediate results will only generate disappointment and conflict. As Bob Woods points out in the book, there are many ways to squeeze costs, but in general, cost-cutting happens at the expense of the plant's future, whereas lean achieves cost savings while improving the plant's capabilities.

On top of all this, many of your colleagues, themselves reluctant to commit to lean, might be watching and waiting for you to fall flat on your face. The upshot is that financial results will eventually come, but never fast enough, and rarely directly connected to one specific lean activity. As the plant gets more "lean", the numbers get better as well. And yes, it is frustrating.

But again, the importance of working with a sensei cannot be understated, in this regard, to keep everyone focused throughout tough times. In the first six months of a lean program, many people are tempted to stop at the low-hanging fruit. Everybody wants a quiet life. And pushing progress beyond the easy initial gains means challenging the status quo-never a good way to make-or even keep-friends. Part of the sensei's job is to stimulate conflict by pushing buttons, uncovering the taboo areas, and systematically challenging the status quo. At the same time he must make sure that conflict remains constructive by proposing avenues for resolving problems, as well as hints and tips. In *The Gold Mine*, Bob Woods takes this tack most of the time. But take note that he too falls into the status quo problem himself, and must be provoked not to become complacent. The first challenge comes from his friend Harry, and the second by his old sensei. The point is that no one is immune to giving in to the frustration and resolving it by reducing expectations, rather than increasing the effort. *The Gold Mine* tries to show that although Bob might come across as formidable to the plant's management team, he's still being needled and coached by his own senseis, at another level.

Q. Can you explain the title?
A. Ah, well, there's a story in that. We were running a lean workshop in India, and the guys were being very clever. They had very good

answers and objections to every lean tool we tried to present. The Indian team members were trying their hardest to understand but simply weren't buying it. Their plant was a clear-cut case of people understanding what we were saying, but not seeing that it applied to them.

As the discussion got increasingly heated, one of the guys called up some data on the inventory around the plant. All these parts had already been sold to customers with signed contracts. And the only way to get the cash out of the customer's pocket was to get the finished product to them as quickly as possible. Surprised and frustrated that his own colleagues couldn't see this, the individual finally exclaimed, "Don't you see-we've got a gold mine in this plant!"

This became the turning point of the workshop. And, we must confess, we did flog the gold mine metaphor to death. But as we began writing the book soon after this work in India, the idea fell in place rather naturally, and we actually use the gold digging metaphor in the book, although not as extensively as the Indian team did.

Q. Please share your background with lean and how it led to this book.

A. This book is the result of the mix of two very different backgrounds. Freddy has been a manufacturing engineer and engineering manager in Renault for about 30 years, and was one of the early Europeans to get interested in the nuts and bolts of the Toyota Production System, or TPS. He realized very early on that this was the only way to compete in the auto industry, and first started to apply individual ideas to production line design as far back as the mid seventies. He got increasingly frustrated by this piecemeal approach as he realized that the Toyota Production System was, well, a system. Eventually, he got the opportunity to deploy the system in full at Valeo as technical vice president. This was one the first implementations of lean as a total production system in Europe.

Freddy then helped the company participate in Toyota's early European supplier integration program, and was trained with a core team of experts by Toyota's own lean gurus from the Operations Management Consulting Division. Finally, as CEO of Sommer Allibert, he had the opportunity to expand lean from lean manufacturing to a total business system. Today he continues to help a number of companies as an independent consultant.

Michael is trained as a sociologist and was researching the cognitive and social roots to "resistance to change" at the time of the early Toyota experiments in Valeo. Following Freddy's advice, he started studying the program in more detail, and caught the lean bug in the process. Michael had previously been working in supply chain dynamic simulations as a consultant with a big six consultancy in London and had published his first book on the topic (*Managing with System Thinking*, McGraw-Hill, 1994). At the time he was looking for practical ways of implementing general systems thinking concepts in practice, and had grown disillusioned with the tack the systems thinking movement was taking at the time. From his point of view, TPS was a revelation: the very embodiment of systems thinking in practice. From this point on, Michael studied the appropriation process of TPS by western companies, and developed his own approach to lean implementation, trying to stick as closely as possible to how Toyota did this with its European suppliers.

The book is the result of Freddy's unusual mix of global and detailed understanding of lean, and Michael's take on lean implementation. Indeed, some technical paragraphs were discussed word by word to get the precise sense right, and in some cases, we believe the book does hold a few previously unpublished nuggets (ah, the gold mine metaphor again). The social and psychological structure to the book is an outgrowth of Michael's research in lean appropriation and implementation. The challenge here is not so much to describe lean, but to propose a workable roadmap to build lean in the culture of the company, which we both believe is the ultimate prize of the lean journey, and which also delivers the pot at the end of the rainbow in terms of financial results.

Q. Many readers who purchase this book are hungry for simple, quick, and easy-to-use tools that will fix their immediate problems. Will this book help them?

A. Every lean tool is quick and easy. We mean it. Again, it's mostly a matter of "just do it". How hard can it be to calculate takt time, draw out a work standard with operators, or talk to operators about how they would improve their workstations? This is, to us, the amazing lesson of many turnarounds. Every tool is easy. The hard part is deciding to use it. Just recently, we've seen a plant manager improve his on-time-in-full delivery rate indicator from a dismal 50% to 95% in one month, just by using takt time! Similarly, a metal stamping plant manager just gained a 10% overall equipment utilization increase on his presses in one week by reacting immediately to every problem, and then went on to stop the weekend shift while maintaining the same production output. The immediate financial gains are dramatic.

The astonishing thing about lean tools is that although everyone moans about how hard they are to implement, occasionally a plant manger wakes up and "just does it." He trains his or her supervisors, and they're off and running, realizing immediate results. The hard thing is staying motivated enough to persevere through the ensuing challenges. In this respect, we hope that *The Gold Mine* can help by giving a realistic description of what to expect in a typical lean journey. As regards quick and easy, the results obtained in *The Gold Mine* are pretty quick, but by all means not as spectacular as some of the things we've seen done. The real question is why these spectacular results don't happen more often.

The Gold Mine should help readers to get a clearer idea of the purpose of each lean tool, and a better expectation of what can happen if you start down the path.

In that respect, we believe the story can help readers realize that their experience at deploying lean is actually more common than they would have thought. In fact, one of the goals of *The Gold Mine* is to bring back lean to "quick and easy" practices on the gemba, and away from large-scale change programs with their consultants, hierarchies and the usual corporate paraphernalia. All too often people tout the "philosophical" aspects of lean (which are fascinating and revolutionary,) but they don't apply it immediately on the shop floor. As Bob Woods would say, "Lean is a practice, not a theory." So let's do it first, see what happens, and figure out how to do it better tomorrow.

A LEAN LEXICON FOR *THE GOLD MINE*

(Adapted from the *Lean Lexicon: a graphical glossary for Lean Thinkers*, 2d edition)

Continuous Flow

Producing and moving one item at a time (or a small and consistent batch of items) through a series of processing steps as continuously as possible, with each step making just what is requested by the next step.

Cycle Time

How often a part or product is completed by a process, as timed by observation. This time includes operating time plus the time required to prepare, load, and unload. Also, the time it takes an operator to go through all work elements before repeating them.

Five S

Five related terms, beginning with an *S* sound, describing workplace practices conducive to visual control and lean production. The five terms in Japanese are:

1. Seiri: Separate needed from unneeded items-tools, parts, materials, paperwork-and discard the unneeded.
2. Seiton: Neatly arrange what is left-a place for everything and everything in its place.
3. Seiso: Clean and wash.
4. Seiketsu: Cleanliness resulting from regular performance of the first three Ss.
5. Shitsuke: Discipline, to perform the first four Ss.

Five Whys

The practice of asking why repeatedly whenever a problem is encountered in order to get beyond the obvious symptoms to discover the root cause.

Heijunka

Leveling the type and quantity of production over a fixed period of time. This enables production to efficiently meet customer demands while avoiding batching and results in minimum inventories, capital costs, manpower, and production lead time through the whole value stream. Roughly, it means "levelization" in Japanese.

Inventory

Materials (and information) present along a value stream between processing steps.

Inventory Turns

A measure of how quickly materials are moving through a facility or through an entire value stream, calculated by dividing some measure of cost of goods by the amount of inventory on hand.

Jidoka

Providing machines and operators the ability to detect when an abnormal condition has occurred and immediately stop work. This enables operations to build in quality at each process and to separate men and machines for more efficient work. Jidoka is one of the two pillars of the Toyota Production System along with just-in-time. It's related to the Japanese word for automation, but with the connotations of humanistic and creating value.

Kaizen

Continuous improvement of an entire value stream or an individual process to create more value with less waste. The word is Japanese for gradual, continuous improvement. There are two levels of kaizen:

1. System or flow kaizen focusing on the overall value stream. This is kaizen for management.

2. Process kaizen focusing on individual processes. This is kaizen for work teams and team leaders.

Kanban
A kanban is a signaling device that gives authorization and instructions for the production or withdrawal (conveyance) of items in a pull system. The term is Japanese for "sign" or "signboard." Kanban cards are the best-known and most common example of these signals.

Muda, Mura, Muri
Three Japanese terms often used together in the Toyota Production System (and called the Three Ms) that collectively describe wasteful practices to be eliminated.

- Muda: Any activity that consumes resources without creating value for the customer.
- Mura: Unevenness in an operation; for example, an uneven work pace in an operation causing operators to hurry and then wait.
- Muri: Overburdening equipment or operators.

Pull Production
A method of production control in which downstream activities signal their needs to upstream activities. Pull production strives to eliminate overproduction and is one of the three major components of a complete just-in-time production system, along with takt time and continuous flow.

Sensei
The Japanese term for "teacher." Used by Lean Thinkers to denote a master of lean knowledge as a result of years of experience.

Seven Wastes

The categorization of the seven major wastes typically found in mass production:

1. Overproduction: Producing ahead of what's actually needed by the next process or customer. The worst form of waste because it contributes to the other six.
2. Waiting: Operators standing idle as machines cycle, equipment fails, needed parts fail to arrive, etc.
3. Conveyance: Moving parts and products unnecessarily, such as from a processing step to a warehouse to a subsequent processing step when the second step instead could be located immediately adjacent to the first step.
4. Processing: Performing unnecessary or incorrect processing, typically from poor tool or product design.
5. Inventory: Having more than the minimum stocks necessary for a precisely controlled pull system.
6. Motion: Operators making movements that are straining or unnecessary, such as looking for parts, tools, documents, etc.
7. Correction: Inspection, rework, and scrap.

Standardized Work

Establishing precise procedures for each operator's work in a production process, based on three elements:

1. Takt time, which is the rate at which products must be made in a process to meet customer demand.
2. The precise work sequence in which an operator performs tasks within takt time.
3. The standard inventory, including units in machines, required to keep the process operating smoothly.

Takt time

The available production time divided by customer demand. For example, if a widget factory operates 480 minutes per day and customers demand 240 widgets per day, takt time is two minutes. *Takt* is German for a precise interval of time.

Total Productive Maintenance

A set of techniques, originally pioneered by Denso in the Toyota Group in Japan, to ensure that every machine in a production process always is able to perform its required tasks.

Value Stream Mapping

A simple diagram of every step involved in the material and information flows needed to bring a product from order to delivery. The first step is to draw a visual representation of every step in a process, including key data, such as the customer demand rate, quality, and machine reliability. Next, draw an improved future-state map showing how the product or service could flow if the steps that add no value were eliminated. Finally, create and implement a plan for achieving the future state.

Waste

Any activity that consumes resources but creates no value for the customer.